Copyright © 2017 by Lenn Vincent GmbH.

All rights reserved. This book or any portion thereof may not be reproduced or used in any manner whatsoever without the express written permission of the publisher except for the use of brief quotations in a book review.

First Printing, 2017

ISBN 978-3-907098-14-1

www.leosnowpard.com

Leo Snowpard
AND HIS FIRST MONEY

Author
MELANIE ROEMER

Illustrations by
JUN-PIERRE SHIOZAWA

"School is over. Yippy!" Leo and his friend Maya dash into the schoolyard. He is very happy because again Maya is allowed to go shopping with him and his dad. Leo always loves it when Maya joins them. Leo's dad is waiting in the parking lot.

"Hello you two. Are you ready for our shopping tour?" His dad greets them. Leo and Maya are happy and jump into the car right away. "Leo, you have to buckle up quickly," urges Maya.

"All strapped?" His dad turns to check, and then off they go.

Arriving at the grocery store, Leo has an idea.

"Maya, let's take our own shopping cart. Then we can shop like our parents. Dad, can we?" asks Leo.

"Ok, that's a great idea. You two can help me to shop," his dad agrees.

Leo and Maya take their own shopping cart. The two find nearly all of the things from the shopping list and put them into the shopping cart.

Then Leo and Maya pass a shelf with bricks. "Hmm, I love bricks," Maya muses. "Me too, but Daddy will surely not buy them for us," Leo replies.
But Maya has an idea. "Pssst," she says to Leo and hides a box beneath the other things in the shopping cart. "No one will notice," she assures Leo.
Leo does not have a good feeling about that. With a bad conscience, he pushes the shopping cart toward the cashier. He knows that his dad does not like it when he does things like this.

Together they begin to place the items on the shopping belt. Leo's dad looks at Maya and Leo with a happy smile. "Thanks for your help that was super quick with you two!" Without much thinking, Leo takes out the box. "Dad, Maya and I wanted to buy these. Can we?" Leo meekly asks. Leo feels bad. He feels like he is kidding his dad.

"No, you two! Leo, I find it great that you were honest with me. But you have enough bricks and besides, these are much too expensive. Please take the box back."

Disappointed and a bit sulky Leo returns the box.

Leo and his dad take Maya home and drive to the workplace of Leo's dad and mom. The two have their own company. Leo does not know what exactly they do at their company. However, he likes being there.

At the company, Leo runs to find his big sister Lilly. Lilly helps mom and dad in the company.

Lilly hears Leo from a distance and is happy to see him. She hugs Leo and then Leo sits down at his usual place at the desk.

"Leo, what did you do today?" Lilly asks.
"Maya and I helped Dad with his shopping. We were much quicker than daddy was. Almost everything was in our shopping cart."
"That sounds great," Lilly says.
"But it was totally cruddy, Lilly. Maya and I wanted to buy some bricks, but Daddy said no. I wish I could just take the things I want! The adults can also do that!"
"Well, Leo that is not correct. At the checkout dad gave the cashier money, right?" Lilly asks.
"I don't know, maybe." Leo murmurs.
"I'm sure Dad paid for the purchase with money. He also can't just take things," Lilly explains.

"Why does money exist?" Leo asks. "Without money everything would be so much easier."

Lilly chuckles. She explains: "If money did not exist, everybody could take what they want. Then nobody would have anything that really belongs to them. For example, Maya could just take your dino book home because it would not be yours."

"But my dino book is mine," Leo replies immediately. Lilly looks at Leo understandingly, "Do you know why your dino book belongs to you?"

Leo thinks. Mom and Dad gave him his dino book as a birthday gift.

"Because Mom and Dad gave it to me for my fifth birthday," Leo replies.

"That's right. They gave you the dino book. But they had to go to the store and buy it."

"You know, Leo, to get your dino book, Mom and Dad exchanged money with the shopkeeper for the book."

"OK, so if I want to buy the bricks, I need money," Leo realizes. "Where do I get money from?"

"You get money when you work. I work here and I get money for it. If I don't work, I have no money. It is the same for Mom and Dad", Lilly explains.

"I would also like to work here", says Leo.

"Sure, you can help me. I'll give you a piece of paper and you go to all the people in the office and tell them to sign it. When you are done, I have more for you to do."

That sounds good, Leo thought, and ran off with the paper.

In the afternoon, it was time to go home.

"Leo, you've been a great help to me today. You will get your money now. Here take these two Pounds."

Leo is very proud of his earning his first money. Lilly asks, "Do you know what you want to do with your two Pounds?" Leo is thinking. "Hmm, if I buy the bricks, my two Pounds are gone, right? Actually, I do still have bricks at home. Do I have to spend my two Pounds?"

"No. If you want, you can save the money until you know what you want to spend them on. You worked for it, so you should think about it carefully."

As soon as Leo reaches home, he immediately runs to his room.
There is a dusty piggy bank hidden in a back corner. He shakes it back and forth. Hmm - it is empty. Then he puts his first money in the piggy bank. From now on, he wants to put all his earnings in there. He will do so until he can buy something he really wants. A new toy? Or... a scooter? Let's see.

www.ingramcontent.com/pod-product-compliance
Lightning Source LLC
Chambersburg PA
CBHW040035050426
42453CB00003B/120

9 783907 098141